Let's Discover Canada

CANADA FACTS AND FIGURES

by
Suzanne LeVert

George Sheppard
McMaster University
General Editor

CHELSEA HOUSE PUBLISHERS

New York   Philadelphia

Cover: The majestic Canadian Rockies
Opposite: The Saddledome arena in Calgary, Alberta

Chelsea House Publishers
EDITOR-IN-CHIEF: Remmel Nunn
MANAGING EDITOR: Karyn Gullen Browne
COPY CHIEF: Mark Rifkin
PICTURE EDITOR: Adrian G. Allen
ART DIRECTOR: Maria Epes
ASSISTANT ART DIRECTOR: Noreen Romano
MANUFACTURING MANAGER: Gerald Levine
SYSTEMS MANAGER: Lindsey Ottman
PRODUCTION MANAGER: Joseph Romano
PRODUCTION COORDINATOR: Marie Claire Cebrián

Let's Discover Canada
SENIOR EDITOR: Rebecca Stefoff

Staff for CANADA FACTS AND FIGURES
SENIOR COPY EDITOR: Laurie Kahn
PICTURE RESEARCHER: Patricia Burns
DESIGNER: Diana Blume

First Printing

1 3 5 7 9 8 6 4 2

Library of Congress Cataloging-in-Publication Data

LeVert, Suzanne.
     Let's discover Canada. Canada, facts and figures/by Suzanne LeVert.
         p.   cm.
     Includes bibliographical references and index.
     Summary: Examines the government, economy, people, provinces, and territories
of Canada.
     ISBN 0-7910-1035-X
     1. Canada—Miscellanea—Juvenile literature.   [1. Canada.]
I. Title.   91-25827
F1008.2.L42   1992   CIP
971—dc20   AC

Contents

My Canada

by Pierre Berton

"Nobody knows my country," a great Canadian journalist, Bruce Hutchison, wrote almost half a century ago. It is still true. Most Americans, I think, see Canada as a pleasant vacationland and not much more. And yet we are the United States's greatest single commercial customer, and the United States is our largest customer.

Lacking a major movie industry, we have made no widescreen epics to chronicle our triumphs and our tragedies. But then there has been little blood in our colonial past—no revolutions, no civil war, not even a wild west. Yet our history is crammed with remarkable men and women. I am thinking of Joshua Slocum, the first man to sail alone around the world, and Robert Henderson, the prospector who helped start the Klondike gold rush. I am thinking of some of our famous artists and writers—comedian Dan Aykroyd, novelists Margaret Atwood and Robertson Davies, such popular performers as Michael J. Fox, Anne Murray, Gordon Lightfoot, and k.d. lang, and hockey greats from Maurice Richard to Gordie Howe to Wayne Gretzky.

The real shape of Canada explains why our greatest epic has been the building of the Pacific Railway to unite the nation from

A cow moose and her young feast on summer's forest bounty in Prince Albert National park in central Saskatchewan.

sea to sea in 1885. On the map, the country looks square. But because the overwhelming majority of Canadians live within 100 miles (160 kilometers) of the U.S. border, in practical terms the nation is long and skinny. We are in fact an archipelago of population islands separated by implacable barriers—the angry ocean, three mountain walls, and the Canadian Shield, that vast desert of billion-year-old rock that sprawls over half the country, rich in mineral treasures, impossible for agriculture.

Canada's geography makes the country difficult to govern and explains our obsession with transportation and communication. The government has to be as involved in railways, airlines, and broadcasting networks as it is with social services such as universal medical care. Rugged individualism is not a Canadian quality. Given the environment, people long ago learned to work together for security.

It is ironic that the very bulwarks that separate us—the chiseled peaks of the Selkirk Mountains, the gnarled scarps north of Lake Superior, the ice-choked waters of the Northumberland Strait —should also be among our greatest attractions for tourists and artists. But if that is the paradox of Canada, it is also the glory.

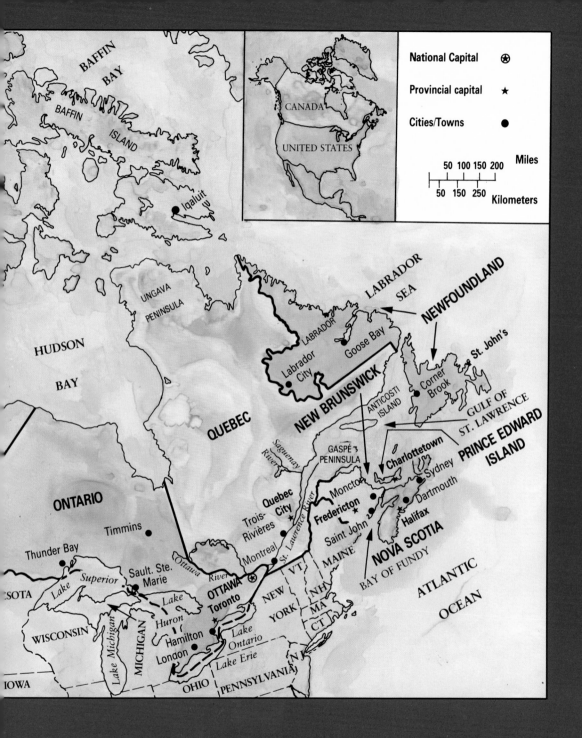

National Capital ⊛

Provincial capital ★

Cities/Towns ●

Miles
50 100 150 200

50 150 250
Kilometers

BAFFIN BAY

BAFFIN ISLAND

Iqaluit

CANADA

UNITED STATES

UNGAVA PENINSULA

HUDSON BAY

LABRADOR SEA

NEWFOUNDLAND

LABRADOR

Goose Bay

Labrador City

St. John's

Corner Brook

GULF OF ST. LAWRENCE

QUEBEC

NEW BRUNSWICK

ANTICOSTI ISLAND

Saguenay River

GASPÉ PENINSULA

Charlottetown

PRINCE EDWARD ISLAND

Sydney

ONTARIO

Moncton

Quebec City

Dartmouth

Trois-Rivières

Fredericton

St. Lawrence River

Timmins

Montreal

Saint John

Halifax

NOVA SCOTIA

Thunder Bay

Ottawa River

MAINE

BAY OF FUNDY

ATLANTIC OCEAN

Sault. Ste. Marie

Lake Superior

OTTAWA
Toronto

VT

NEW YORK

NH

MA

CSOTA

Lake Michigan

Lake Huron

Hamilton

Lake Ontario

CT

WISCONSIN

MICHIGAN

London

Lake Erie

N

IOWA

OHIO

PENNSYLVANIA

Chronology

1000	Viking Leif Eriksson lands in Vinland, probably at the site now called L'Anse-aux-Meadows in Newfoundland.
1497	Navigator John Cabot explores Canada's east coast.
1534	Jacques Cartier explores the Gulf of St. Lawrence; landing on Quebec's Gaspé Peninsula, he claims the land for France.
1583	Humphrey Gilbert claims Newfoundland for Britain.
1608	French explorer Samuel de Champlain founds the city of Quebec.
1610	British explorer Henry Hudson discovers Hudson Bay.
1642	Ville-Marie de Montréal, later shortened to Montreal, is founded by French missionaries.
1670	A British trading firm called the Hudson's Bay Company is founded and given title to much of northern and central Canada.
1713	Under the Treaty of Utrecht, France surrenders to Britain its claims to Hudson Bay, Newfoundland, and most of eastern Canada.
1755	The British forcibly expel the Acadians (settlers of French descent) from Nova Scotia and New Brunswick.
1759	British forces under General James Wolfe defeat French troops on the Plains of Abraham outside Quebec City.
1763	The Treaty of Paris ends decades of fighting between the French and British in both Europe and Canada. France gives its North American territory (except the small islands of St. Pierre and Miquelon in the Gulf of St. Lawrence) to Britain.

1774   The Quebec Act gives French Canadians political rights and religious freedom under British rule.

1789   Explorer Alexander Mackenzie follows the Mackenzie River from central Canada to the Arctic coast.

1807   Explorers David Thompson and Simon Fraser travel through what is now British Columbia.

1812   During the War of 1812 between the United States and Britain, many battles are fought in British North America (Canada). The British, French Canadians, and Native Americans are allies against U.S. forces.

1837   Factions in Quebec and Ontario rebel against the colonial government; the rebellions are crushed, but a British investigation results in greater independence for the Canadian colonies.

1840   The Act of Union unites Canada West (Ontario) and Canada East (Quebec) into the province of Canada, with a new parliament.

1848   The provinces of Canada and Nova Scotia gain self-government.

1857   Queen Victoria names Bytown (now Ottawa) the capital of Canada.

1864   Colonial leaders meet at Charlottetown, Prince Edward Island, to discuss creating the nation of Canada.

1867   Nova Scotia, New Brunswick, Quebec, and Ontario unite in a confederation called the Dominion of Canada. Sir John A. Macdonald is named Canada's first prime minister.

1869   Canada buys the western lands from the Hudson's Bay Company. In Manitoba, Louis Riel leads an uprising of Métis (people of mixed French and Native descent) against British rule. The rebellion is quickly crushed.

Bygone battles are reenacted during historical festivals on Citadel Hill in Halifax, Nova Scotia. Britain and France fought over ownership of the colonies in Nova Scotia and other parts of Canada for much of the 17th and 18th centuries.

A railway snakes through British Columbia's Yoho National Park. Canada's first transcontinental railway, completed in 1885, played a crucial part in the opening of the Canadian west to commerce and settlement.

1870	The province of Manitoba is made part of the Dominion of Canada; the North West Territories is established.
1871	The province of British Columbia is added to the Dominion of Canada.
1873	The province of Prince Edward Island is added to the Dominion of Canada.
1885	The last spike is driven in Canada's transcontinental railway. Louis Riel leads a Métis revolt in Saskatchewan; he is captured and executed.
1896	Gold is discovered near the Klondike River in the Yukon district of the North West Territories, spurring the Klondike gold rush.
1898	The Yukon is given territorial status.
1905	The provinces of Saskatchewan and Alberta are added to the Dominion of Canada.
1926	Britain's Balfour Declaration recognizes autonomy for former British colonies, including Canada.
1931	The Statute of Westminster gives Canada complete independence from Great Britain.
1947	Oil is discovered at Leduc, Alberta; Canada's oil industry begins large-scale development.
1949	Newfoundland becomes Canada's 10th province. Canada, the United States, and 10 western European nations form the North Atlantic Treaty Organization (NATO).
1959	The St. Lawrence Seaway, a joint U.S.-Canadian project, opens, allowing oceangoing ships to reach the Great Lakes.
1962	The Trans-Canada Highway, the nation's first ocean-to-ocean automobile route, is completed.
1965	The National Health Plan is introduced.

1967   Canada hosts Expo 67, a world's fair, to celebrate its 100th anniversary.

1970   A separatist movement called the Front de Libération Québecois (FLQ) kidnaps and kills Pierre Laporte, Quebec's minister of labor; the government responds by declaring the War Measures Act and arresting 500 Quebec separatists.

1976   Montreal hosts the Summer Olympics. The Parti Québecois, which advocates independence for Quebec, wins a majority in the National Assembly.

1980   Three-fifths of the people of Quebec vote to remain in Canada.

1982   Canada adopts a new constitution that ends British control over constitutional amendments; a Charter of Rights and Freedoms is added.

1989   Canada and the United States enact a free-trade agreement that will eliminate all tariffs on goods transported between the two countries by 1998.

1990   The Meech Lake Accord, which would have given Quebec special status within the Dominion of Canada, fails to become law.

Provinces and Territories Ranked by Population and Area

	Population	Area		Population	Area
Alberta	4	7	Nova Scotia	7	11
British Columbia	3	4	Ontario	1	3
Manitoba	5	6	Prince Edward Island	10	12
New Brunswick	8	10	Quebec	2	2
Newfoundland	9	9	Saskatchewan	6	5
Northwest Territories	11	1	Yukon	12	8

Left: Inuit on the shores of Baker Lake in the Northwest Territories. The Inuit, many of whom live above the Arctic Circle, are the continent's northernmost indigenous people.

Opposite: Founded in the 1640s by French Catholic missionaries, Montreal is today the largest city in Canada. It is also a major center of business, trade, and the arts.

Canada at a Glance

Area: 3,851,790 square miles (9,978,653 square kilometers)

Highest point: Mt. Logan, 19,850 feet (5,951 meters)

Population: 25,354,064 (in 1986 census); estimated 1990 population 26,279,000

Population density: 6 people per square mile (2 per square kilometer)

Population distribution: Urban 76 percent, rural 24 percent

Languages spoken: 60.6 percent English, 24.3 percent French, 11.3 percent other, 3.8 percent bilingual

Capital: Ottawa (pop. 300,763)

Major cities: Montreal (pop. 1,054,420), Calgary (pop. 636,100), Toronto (pop. 612,290), Winnipeg (pop. 594,551), Edmonton (pop. 574,000), Vancouver (pop. 420,000)

National anthem: "O Canada"

National motto: *A mari usque ad mare* (From sea to sea)

Coat of arms: Three maple leaves below the royal arms of England, Scotland, Ireland, and France

National flag: Red and white stripes with a stylized red maple leaf

National symbols: Maple leaf and beaver

Currency: Canadian dollar

Chief exports: Wheat and other agricultural products, newsprint and other paper products, lumber, petroleum, natural gas, iron, chemicals, textiles, transportation equipment

Gross domestic product: Services 63 percent, industry 33 percent, agriculture 4 percent

Per capita income: Equivalent to U.S. $13,000

Special features: Canada is the second largest country in the world in area, after the Soviet Union, but 31st in population. Larger than the United States, it has about one-tenth of the population of the United States.

Left: People of Ukrainian descent are numerous in Alberta and the other prairie provinces. In the town of Vegreville, a center of Ukrainian Canadian culture, they celebrate Easter in traditional dress.

Opposite: Peyto Lake, Banff National Park, in the Canadian Rocky Mountains. Its magnificent wilderness scenery is one of Alberta's most valuable resources; others include oil fields and prime agricultural land.

Alberta at a Glance

Area: 225,285 square miles (661,185 square kilometers)

Highest point: Mt. Columbia 12,294 feet (3,725 meters)

Major rivers: Peace, Slave, Athabasca, North Saskatchewan, South Saskatchewan, Red Deer

Major lakes: Lesser Slave, Claire, Athabasca

Population: 2,365,825 (in 1986 census)

Population density: 9 people per square mile (4 per square kilometer)

Population distribution: Urban 77 percent, rural 23 percent

Languages spoken: 81 percent English, 2.1 percent French, 13.3 percent other (including German 3.2 percent, Ukrainian 2.0 percent), 3.6 percent bilingual

Capital: Edmonton (pop. 574,000)

Other cities: Calgary (pop. 636,100), Lethbridge (pop. 59,000), Red Deer (pop. 52,000)

Entered Dominion of Canada: September 1, 1905

Provincial motto: *Fortis et liber* (Strong and free)

Provincial flower: Wild rose (also known as prickly rose)

Provincial bird: Great horned owl

Provincial coat of arms: The Cross of St. George, representing Alberta's link with Great Britain; a landscape with mountains, a prairie, and a field of wheat

Principal products: Oil, natural gas, wheat

Gross domestic product: Services 59 percent, industry 37 percent, agriculture 4 percent

Special features: Nicknamed the Sunshine Province for its clear blue skies and temperate climate. The only province in which all three of Canada's dominant landforms—the rocky Canadian Shield of the north, the High Plains of the interior, and the mountain ranges of the west—are represented. Has the world's largest shopping center, the West Edmonton Mall.

Left: Vancouver is British Columbia's largest city. It is home to many ethnic groups, including a large concentration of Asian Canadians.

Opposite: The forests of British Columbia flourish in the province's mild coastal temperatures and high rainfall. Among the oldest and thickest woodlands of North America, they have become the subject of heated debates between loggers and conservationists.

British Columbia at a Glance

Area: 365,255 square miles (946,011 square kilometers)

Highest point: Mt. Fairweather, 15,300 feet (4,633 meters)

Major rivers: Fraser, Columbia, Skeena

Population: 3,029,000 (in 1986 census)

Population density: 7 people per square mile (3 per square kilometer)

Population distribution: Urban 79 percent, rural 21 percent

Languages spoken: 80.9 percent English, 1.4 percent French, 14.5 percent other (primarily Chinese and Southeast Asian languages), 3.2 percent bilingual

Capital: Victoria (pop. 65,000)

Other cities: Vancouver (pop. 420,000), Surrey (pop. 181,500)

Entered Dominion of Canada: July 20, 1871

Provincial motto: *Splendor sine occasu* (Splendor without diminishment)

Provincial flower: Pacific dogwood

Provincial bird: Steller's jay

Provincial coat of arms: Wavy blue lines represent the Pacific Ocean; the setting sun symbolizes British Columbia's location as the westernmost province; and the royal lion, crown, and Union Jack symbolize the province's ties with Great Britain

Principal products: Lumber, pulp-and-paper products, processed foods, livestock, primary metals

Gross domestic product: Services 72 percent, industry 24 percent, agriculture 4 percent

Special features: Canada's most geographically diverse province, with dense rainforests as well as the country's only true desert. More than 90 percent of land is owned by the provincial government. Province is larger than all but 30 nations in the world. Vancouver's Stanley Park is one of the biggest urban parks in North America, at more than 1,000 acres (400 hectares).

Left: Manitoba is considered a prairie province, along with Saskatchewan and Alberta. Wheat fields and grain elevators are familiar features on the landscape in the southwestern part of the province.

Opposite: A polar bear near Churchill, Manitoba, searches a strand of seaweed for anything edible. One of the world's largest concentrations of these huge mammals lives in the vicinity of Churchill, which calls itself the Polar Bear Capital of the World.

Manitoba at a Glance

Area: 251,000 square miles (650,087 square kilometers)
Highest point: Mt. Baldy, 2,279 feet (832 meters)
Major rivers: Churchill
Major lakes: Winnipeg, Manitoba
Population: 1,063,016 (in 1986 census)
Population density: 4 people per square mile (2 per square kilometer)
Population distribution: Urban 72 percent, rural 28 percent
Languages spoken: 71.3 percent English, 4.3 percent French, 18.6 percent other, 5.8 percent bilingual
Capital: Winnipeg (pop. 594,551)
Other cities: Brandon (pop. 38,708), Thompson (pop. 14,701) Portage-la-Prairie (pop. 13,198)
Entered Dominion of Canada: July 15, 1870

Provincial flower: Pasqueflower
Provincial bird: Grey owl
Provincial coat of arms: A buffalo represents the province's early history; the Cross of St. George represents Manitoba's ties to Great Britain
Principal products: Wheat, nickel, petroleum
Gross domestic product: Services 73 percent, industry 20 percent, agriculture 7 percent
Special features: Nicknamed the Keystone Province (also the Gateway to the West), Manitoba lies at the center of the nation, linking eastern Canada to the prairies of the interior and the mountains of the west. Has the only seaport in the prairie provinces (at Churchill). Churchill is also one of the world's largest denning areas for polar bears.

Left: The valley of the Saint John River is a tranquil farming region in New Brunswick. The terrain in other parts of the province is more rugged and heavily forested.

Opposite: Fishermen on Grand Manan Island pull in their catch.

New Brunswick at a Glance

Area: 28,354 square miles (73,437 square kilometers)

Highest point: Mt. Carleton, 2,690 feet (820 meters)

Major rivers: Saint John, Miramichi

Population: 710,442 (in 1986 census)

Population density: 25 people per square mile (10 per square kilometer)

Population distribution: Urban 51 percent, rural 49 percent

Languages spoken: 68 percent English, 31.4 percent French, 0.6 percent other (European and Asian)

Capital: Fredericton (pop. 44,352)

Other cities: Saint John (pop. 76,381), Moncton (pop. 55,468), Bathurst (pop. 14,683)

Entered Dominion of Canada: July 1, 1867

Provincial motto: *Spem reduxit* (Hope was restored)

Provincial flower: Purple violet

Provincial bird: Black-capped chickadee

Provincial coat of arms: A lion symbolizes New Brunswick's ties with Great Britain; a galley represents the importance of shipbuilding and seafaring; a salmon forms the crest; two white-tailed deer support the shield

Principal products: Lumber and other forestry products, potatoes, lead

Gross domestic product: Services 72 percent, industry 22 percent, agriculture 6 percent

Special features: Nicknamed the Picture Province for its striking landscape and scenery. One of four Atlantic provinces (with Newfoundland, Prince Edward Island, and Nova Scotia) and one of three Maritime provinces (with Prince Edward Island and Nova Scotia). The heart of Acadia, the original French settlement in North America.

Left: The docks at Goose Bay in Labrador

Opposite: Petty Harbour is one of many small coastal communities called outports. Some outports can be reached only by water, and many Newfoundlanders are as much at home in small boats as in automobiles.

Newfoundland at a Glance

Area: 156,185 square miles (404,517 square kilometers)

Highest point: Torngat Mountains, 5,500 feet (1,667 meters)

Population: 568,349 (in 1986 census)

Population density: 4 people per square mile (2 per square kilometer)

Population distribution: Urban 59 percent, rural 41 percent

Languages spoken: English 98.6 percent, French 0.4 percent, other 0.7 percent, 0.3 percent bilingual

Capital: St. John's (pop. 96,216)

Other cities: Corner Brook (pop. 22,719), Mount Pearl (pop. 20,293), Labrador City (pop. 8,664)

Entered Dominion of Canada: March 31, 1949

Provincial motto: *Quaerite prime regnum dei* (Seek ye first the kingdom of God)

Provincial flower: Pitcher plant

Provincial bird: Atlantic puffin

Provincial coat of arms: Red shield with white cross, with two lions and two unicorns, with figures of Native Americans on either side and an elk on top

Principal products: Fish, forestry products, iron ore

Gross domestic product: Services 70 percent, industry 27 percent, agriculture 3 percent

Special features: Province consists of two parts, Newfoundland Island and part of the Labrador Peninsula on the Canadian mainland. Newfoundland Island was England's first possession in North America, claimed by Sir Humphrey Gilbert in 1583. Guglielmo Marconi received the first transatlantic radio message at St. John's on December 12, 1901. The Churchill Falls hydroelectric power plant, which has 11 generators, is one of the largest power plants in the Western Hemisphere.

Left: The population of the Northwest Territories includes a high percentage of Native Americans.

Opposite: Lee Point, Ellesmere Island. The Northwest Territories stretches toward the North Pole and includes many Arctic islands, of which Ellesmere is the farthest north.

Northwest Territories at a Glance

Area: 1,304,895 square miles (3,379,684 square kilometers), 33.9 percent of Canada's total area

Highest point: Mt. Sir James MacBrien, 9,062 feet (2,762 meters)

Population: 52,238 (in 1986 census), .21 percent of Canada's population

Population density: 4 persons per 100 square miles (2 per 100 square kilometers)

Population distribution: Rural 52 percent, urban 48 percent

Languages spoken: 53.6 percent English, 27.8 percent Inuktitut (a Native American language), 2.5 percent French, 16.1 percent other

Capital: Yellowknife (pop. 11,753)

Other cities: Inuvik (pop. 3,389), Hay River (pop. 2,964), Iqaluit (pop. 2,947)

Entered Dominion of Canada: July 15, 1870

Provincial flower: Mountain avens

Provincial bird: Gyrfalcon

Provincial coat of arms: A wavy blue line represents the Northwest Passage; gold bars symbolize mineral wealth; a white fox symbolizes the fur industry; and two narwhals (Arctic whales) guard a compass rose, which symbolizes the magnetic North Pole

Principal products: Fish, petroleum, zinc, gold

Special features: The largest portion of Canada, with the second lowest population of any province or territory. Includes many islands in the Arctic Ocean. Contains Canada's longest river, the Mackenzie, and two of its largest lakes, Great Slave Lake and Great Bear Lake. The scene of exploration in search of the Northwest Passage from the 16th through 19th centuries. Home of two Native American cultures: the Dene peoples of the forest and the Inuit peoples of the tundra, the Arctic coast, and the Arctic islands.

Left: Recreational fishing is one of the major attractions of Nova Scotia, for residents and tourists alike.

Opposite: Nova Scotia's Atlantic coast has been carved by the sea into countless bays, coves, and harbors. These sheltered anchorages have been the sites of fishing settlements for hundreds of years.

Nova Scotia at a Glance

Area: 21,423 square miles (55,490 square kilometers)

Highest point: North Barren, 1,747 feet (532 meters), in Cape Breton National Highlands

Major rivers: St. Mary's, Shubenacadie

Major lakes: Bras d'Or

Population: 873,199 (in 1986 census)

Population density: 40 people per square mile (15 per square kilometers)

Population distribution: Urban 55 percent, rural 45 percent

Languages spoken: 93.2 English, 3.5 percent French, 1.8 percent other, 1.5 percent bilingual

Capital: Halifax (pop. 113,577)

Other cities: Dartmouth (pop. 65,243), Sydney (pop. 27,754), Glace Bay (pop. 20,467)

Entered Dominion of Canada: July 1, 1867

Provincial motto: *Munit haec et altera vincit* (One defends and the other conquers)

Provincial flower: Trailing arbutus (also called mayflower)

Provincial coat of arms: The Cross of St. Andrew and the arms of Scotland represent Scottish heritage; a Native American represents the original inhabitants; a unicorn symbolizes England

Principal products: Milk, hogs, lobsters, paper products, coal, gypsum

Gross domestic product: Services 74 percent, industry 23 percent, agriculture 3 percent

Special features: Province consists of two parts: the end of a mainland peninsula and a nearby island. First airplane flight in Canada was made in Nova Scotia in 1909; first newspaper in Canada was the Halifax *Gazette*, started in 1752; first regular mail service by steamship between Great Britain, Canada, and the United States was established by Samuel Cunard of Halifax.

Left: The changing of the guard ceremony outside Parliament in Ottawa is an echo of British tradition.

Opposite: Toronto, Ontario's largest city and capital, glitters by night. The most distinctive feature of the city's skyline is the freestanding spire of the Canadian National (CN) Tower.

Ontario at a Glance

Area: 412,582 square miles (1,068,582 square kilometers)

Highest point: Ogidaki Mountain, 2,183 feet (662 meters)

Major rivers: Ottawa, St. Lawrence, Thames, Albany

Population: 9,101,694 (in 1986 census)

Population density: 21 people per square mile (8 per square kilometer)

Population distribution: Urban 86 percent, rural 14 percent

Languages spoken: 76 percent English, 5 percent French, 19 percent other

Capital: Toronto (pop. 612,290)

Other cities: North York (pop. 556,297), Scarborough (pop. 484,674), Hamilton (pop. 400,000), Ottawa (pop. 300,763)

Entered Dominion of Canada: July 1, 1867

Provincial motto: *Ut inceptit fideles sic permanent* (Loyal she began, loyal she remains)

Provincial flower: White trillium (also called white lily)

Provincial bird: Common loon (under consideration)

Provincial coat of arms: The Cross of St. George symbolizes the province's ties to Great Britain; three maple leaves symbolize Canada

Principal products: Transportation equipment, food products, nickel, gold, beef cattle, tobacco

Gross domestic product: Services 64 percent, industry 34 percent, agriculture 2 percent

Special features: Known as Canada's Heartland—rich in resources and vast in size. One of the original four founding colonies of the Dominion of Canada. The seat of Canada's federal government, which is located in Ottawa. Insulin was discovered at the University of Toronto in 1921. The CN (Canadian National) Tower in Toronto is the world's tallest freestanding structure at 1,815 feet (533 meters).

Left: Canada's smallest province contains fertile farmland and good pasture for livestock.

Opposite: Near Tignish, at the northern tip of the island, an algae called Irish moss is harvested from the Gulf of St. Lawrence.

Prince Edward Island at a Glance

Area: 2,184 square miles (5,657 square kilometers)

Highest point: 465 feet (125 meters) in Queens County

Population: 126,646 (in 1986 census)

Population density: 56 people per square mile (22 per square kilometer)

Population distribution: Rural 64 percent, urban 36 percent

Languages spoken: 96.6 percent English; 3 percent French; 0.4 percent other

Capital: Charlottetown (pop. 15,776)

Other cities: Summerside (pop. 7,500)

Entered Dominion of Canada: July 1, 1873

Provincial motto: *Parva sub ingenti* (The small under the protection of the great)

Provincial flower: Lady slipper

Provincial bird: Blue jay

Provincial tree: Northern red oak

Provincial coat of arms: The upper third is a field of red on which there is a gold lion; the lower two-thirds are white with one large and three small green oaks

Principal products: Potatoes, lobsters, printed materials, wood products

Gross domestic product: Services 73 percent, industry 14 percent, agriculture 13 percent

Special features: Irish moss, Canada's most commercially valuable seaweed, is harvested off Prince Edward Island and used to make soap, fertilizer, and other products. Prince Edward Island is the setting for *Anne of Green Gables*, a well-loved children's book by Lucy Maud Montgomery, a native of the province.

Left: Quebec City, the province's capital, is a bastion of French language, culture, and architecture. The oldest parts of the city have been designated a World Heritage Site by the United Nations.

Opposite: Mont Tremblant, in the Laurentian Mountains of south-central Quebec, is a popular ski resort. The vast northern part of the province consists of tundra and waterways and is sparsely populated.

Quebec at a Glance

Area: 594,860 square miles (1,500,000 square kilometers)
Highest point: Mt. Jacques Cartier, 4,160 feet (1,260 meters)
Major rivers: St. Lawrence, Saguenay
Population: 6.5 million (in 1986 census)
Population density: 11 people per square mile (4 per square kilometer)
Population distribution: Urban 78 percent, rural 22 percent
Languages spoken: 81.9 percent French, 8.9 percent English, 9.2 percent other
Capital: Quebec City (pop. 164,580)
Other cities: Montreal (pop. 1,015,420), Laval (pop. 284,441)
Entered Dominion of Canada: July 1, 1867
Provincial motto: *Je me souviens* (I remember)

Provincial flower: Madonna lily
Provincial bird: Snowy owl
Provincial coat of arms: Combines emblems of France (fleur de lis), Great Britain (lion), and Canada (maple leaf)
Principal products: Pulp-and-paper products, food processing products, automobiles and transport equipment, gold, iron ore, asbestos
Gross domestic product: Services 68 percent, industry 29 percent, agriculture 3 percent
Special features: Nicknamed the Storied Province because of its colorful history. One of the four original provinces to unite in confederation. About 80 percent of the province's population is of French ancestry; Quebec City and Montreal are the focus of French language and culture in Canada.

Left: The cowboy heritage of the prairies lives on in rodeos. Almost every town in western Canada has a rodeo in the summer or fall.

Opposite: Saskatchewan is Canada's Breadbasket, with 40 percent of the country's farmland. Its huge wheat harvests are stored in thousands of grain elevators and shipped by rail to distant markets and ports.

Saskatchewan at a Glance

Area: 251,700 square miles (651,942 square kilometers)

Highest point: Cypress Hills, 4,546 feet (1,386 meters)

Major rivers: Saskatchewan, South Saskatchewan, North Saskatchewan, Churchill, Qu'Appelle

Major lakes: Athabasca, Wollaston, Wathaman

Population: 1,009,000 (in 1986 census)

Population density: 4 people per square mile (2 per square kilometer)

Population distribution: Urban 58 percent, rural 42 percent

Languages spoken: 92.8 percent English, 1 percent French, 6.2 percent other

Capital: Regina (pop. 175,000)

Other cities: Saskatoon (pop. 177,000), Moose Jaw (pop. 35,000), Prince Albert (pop. 34,000)

Entered Dominion of Canada: September 1, 1905

Provincial flower: Western red lily (also called prairie lily)

Provincial bird: Sharp-tailed grouse

Provincial coat of arms: Three sheaves of wheat on a green background represent agriculture; a red lion on a yellow background represents loyalty to the British crown

Principal products: Wheat, beef cattle, food products, machinery, petroleum

Gross domestic product: Services 65 percent, industry 21 percent, agriculture 14 percent

Special features: Known as Canada's Breadbasket because it includes two-fifths of the country's farmland, more than any other province. Had first elected socialist government in North America in 1944. Introduced many of Canada's social programs, including state-funded health care.

Left: A camp in the southern Yukon. The small hut on stilts (left of center) is a cache designed to keep food out of the reach of bears.

Opposite: Dogsledding, developed by the Natives into a highly efficient form of transportation over winter snows, has become a major sport in Canada's far north.

Yukon Territory at a Glance

Area: 186,299 square miles (482,515 square kilometers), 4.9 percent of Canada's area

Highest point: Mt. Logan, 19,850 feet (5,591 meters)

Major rivers: Yukon, Klondike, Peel, Porcupine

Population: 23,504 (in 1986 census)

Population density: 13 people per 100 square miles (5 per 100 square kilometers)

Population distribution: Urban 64 percent, rural 36 percent

Languages spoken: 90 percent English, 2.5 percent French, 7.5 percent other

Capital: Whitehorse (pop. 15,199)

Other cities: Dawson City (pop. 896), Watson Lake (pop. 826)

Entered Dominion of Canada: June 13, 1898

Provincial flower: Fireweed, a member of the evening primrose family

Provincial bird: Raven

Provincial coat of arms: The Cross of St. George represents British explorers; a circle symbolizes the fur trade; red triangles with gold circles represent the Yukon's mineral-rich mountains; wavy stripes represent its river

Principal products: Lead, zinc, gold, lumber

Special features: The site of North America's largest gold rush after gold was found near the Klondike River in 1898. A major World War II construction project, the Alaska Highway, crosses the southern Yukon. Known for extremely cold temperatures; one of the coldest temperatures ever recorded in North America, -81°F (-63°C), was recorded at Snag Airport near the Alaskan border in 1947.

Canada's Government

The nation of Canada was born in 1867. That year, the British Parliament, at the request of four colonies in North America, passed the British North America Act (BNA). The act created a largely independent confederation of four provinces, Quebec, Ontario, Nova Scotia, and New Brunswick. Over the years, six additional provinces and two territories have joined the original four to form today's Canada.

Canada maintains close ties with Great Britain as a member of the Commonwealth of Nations, an association of Great Britain and its former colonies. Canada recognizes the British monarch, Queen Elizabeth II, as its formal head of state, and Canada's style of government is modeled largely on the British parliamentary system.

In establishing the Dominion of Canada, the BNA—now known as the Constitution Act of 1867—provided for a separation of federal and provincial or territorial powers. The federal government was given control of such areas as defense, customs, and currency—in general, areas that involve international affairs or the interests of the whole country. The provinces received control of education, natural resources, civil

Opposite: The Houses of Parliament in Ottawa, where the Senate and the House of Commons meet to govern the nation.
Above: Brian Mulroney, Canada's prime minister, is head of the country's government.

The provincial legislature of Ontario in Toronto. Each province and territory has its own legislature and head of government.

rights, municipal government, and other matters of local concern. In certain areas—agriculture, immigration, and taxation—the two levels of government were granted joint power.

Although the Constitution Act of 1867 laid the foundation for the Canadian government, it does not form the entire constitution. In fact, Canada's body of laws and system of government consist of both written and unwritten codes. The basic written section is the Constitution Act of 1982, which includes the BNA.

The unwritten codes of Canada's constitution include the parliamentary cabinet system of government, patterned after the one used in Great Britain. The cabinet system links two of the three main branches of government, the executive and legislative, on both the federal and provincial levels. The prime minister and his executive officers are usually members of the political party that holds a majority of the seats in the House of Commons, the main body of the legislature. The third branch of government, the judiciary, is an appointed body and is not tied to the election of a particular party.

Members of the House of Commons are elected by popular vote in general elections. Canadian citizens, age 18 or older, may vote in national elections. Each province sets its own voting requirements for provincial elections; most have a voting age of 18.

The government's executive branch is composed of the monarch, the prime minister, and the cabinet. The monarch's representative in Canada is the governor-general, a Canadian who is formally appointed by the queen on the advice of the Canadian government. The governor-general has little power and acts in a formal and ceremonial manner only.

The real executive power in Canada is held by the prime minister and his or her cabinet. The prime minister is the leader of the party that has a majority of seats in the House of Commons. The prime minister chooses a cabinet, usually from among members of the same party in the House of Commons and at least one member of the Senate. The cabinet ministers run the various departments of government—National Defence,

External Affairs, Finance, Public Works and Transportation, among others—and together they shape government policy for the nation as a whole. There is no sharp distinction between the executive and legislative branches in Canada. The prime minister and almost all of the cabinet ministers are also members of the House of Commons, and the government can remain in office only as long as it has the support of a majority of members of the legislature. If the Commons defeats a government bill or successfully passes a motion of nonconfidence, the prime minister must resign or dissolve parliament and face the people in an election.

To get laws passed, the cabinet presents proposals to both houses of parliament. The House of Commons, consisting of 282 elected members, must approve all legislation before it can be enacted.

The Senate has 104 members, selected by the prime minister and cabinet. The Senate can reject a bill, but has not done so for nearly 30 years. It can also amend any bill.

The provincial governments are similar to the federal government, except that none of the provinces has a Senate. A lieutenant governor (appointed by the governor-general on the recommendation of the prime minister) represents the queen in each province but has duties that are largely ceremonial. A premier heads the government of each province. Each premier is the leader of the majority party in that province's legislature. Each province has an elected one-chamber legislature called the Legislative Assembly, except in Quebec, where it is called the National Assembly.

Canada's far north is divided into two territories: the Yukon and the Northwest Territories. These territories have separate governments with far less power than those of the provinces. Although the autonomous powers of the two territorial governments have gradually increased over several decades, the territories still largely fall under the jurisdiction of the federal government and parliament. They are headed by officials called government leaders, the leaders of their legislative assemblies.

Canada's Economy

Canada is a nation rich in natural resources. It also has a highly educated and skilled work force. Measured in terms of gross domestic product (GDP)—the total value of goods and services produced by a country in a year—Canada's economy ranks among the top 10 in the world. It is also one of the most diversified.

Manufacturing industries make up one of the largest sectors of the Canadian economy, accounting for about 19 percent of the GDP and 16 percent of all employment. Ontario and Quebec together produce more than three-fourths of Canada's manufactured goods.

Forestry provides Canada with its largest manufacturing sector in terms of income, employment, and wages. The world's largest exporter of forest products, Canada accounts for 22 percent of all forest products traded in world markets. It is the world's third largest producer of paper and the leading producer of newsprint (the paper upon which newspapers are printed). British Columbia, Quebec, and Ontario together account for about 88 percent of the forest industry's output.

Minerals, including oil, are among the country's most important resources. In 1989, the value of Canada's mineral production totaled more than $39 billion. Canada is a major

Opposite: St. John's, Newfoundland, is one of Atlantic Canada's major seaports.
Above: The Thetford Mines in Quebec. Canada is one of the world's leading producers of minerals.

producer of a wide variety of minerals, including nickel, zinc, copper, gold, iron ore, potash, uranium, sulphur, asbestos, silver, and titanium.

Canada is also a leading exporter of petroleum and natural gas. The petroleum industry extracted approximately $16 billion worth of products in 1988; the province of Alberta accounted for 87 percent of the value of all crude oil, natural gas, and gas by-products.

Although the number of farms and farmers is declining, agriculture still plays a significant role in Canada's economy and is an important part of foreign trade. In 1988, total net farm income was $3.5 billion. Exports of agricultural products accounted for about 8 percent of all export sales that year.

Wheat is Canada's dominant crop, in terms of both production and export value. In 1989, 24 million tons of wheat were produced. Canada also grows about $1 billion worth of a wide variety of fruits and vegetables each year. The most important fruit crop is apples. British Columbia's Okanagan Valley is also a source of pears, peaches, cherries, plums, and grapes. Alberta is the country's leading producer of beef cattle. Farmers in Alberta, Manitoba, and Saskatchewan—the prairie provinces—also raise dairy cows, hogs, and poultry.

Canada's commercial fishing industry is one of the largest in the world. Approximately 93,000 commercial fishermen in 36,000 vessels ply Canada's coastal waters as well as its lakes and rivers. In 1988, the catch totaled 1.63 million tons and was valued at $1.64 billion.

Canada is one of the leading international trading nations. Its imports and exports total more than $250 billion annually. In 1988, exports exceeded imports by nearly $10 billion. Major exports include automobiles and automobile parts, chemicals, aluminum, fish, lumber, natural gas, newsprint, petroleum, wheat, and wood pulp. Imports include computers, electrical appliances, fruits and vegetables, and scientific instruments.

Canada's major trading partner is the United States. In 1988, trade with the United States accounted for 73 percent ($98 billion) of domestic exports and 65 percent ($86 billion) of imports. In 1989, Canada and the United States signed a joint free-trade agreement that will eliminate all tariffs and other restrictions on trade between the 2 nations over a 10-year period. Some economists believe that the agreement will increase the volume of trade, increase employment, and raise real income in both countries. Others in Canada, however, feel that the agreement favors the United States. Taxes and property values are generally lower in the United States, which means that it is often less expensive to manufacture or purchase goods there than in Canada. Many Canadian companies have shifted their operations to the United States. Nearly 300,000 Canadian manufacturing jobs have been eliminated since 1989, and many Canadians feel that the free-trade agreement is at least partly to blame.

Like many other industrialized nations, Canada entered the 1990s in an economic recession. The unemployment rate hit a 10-year high of more than 10 percent, consumers were spending less money on goods and services, and more manufacturing industries were closing. Canadian citizens also faced high taxes: In 1991, taxes in Canada were among the highest in the industrialized world.

Although high taxes reduce the amount of money available for consumer spending, they help pay for social services. Canada has one of the most comprehensive social health and welfare programs in the world. Health services are provided free of charge to all Canadians who need them.

Although Canadians have long been proud of these compassionate social programs, they are now reexamining the cost attached to them in the form of high taxes. Balancing the costs with the benefits of these programs is one of Canada's most pressing economic challenges. Other challenges Canada faces include recovering from the recession, strengthening the manufacturing sector, protecting the environment from the destructive effects of economic development, and competing with the United States, Mexico, Japan, and other trading partners. Despite these formidable challenges, Canada's wealth of natural resources and its skilled labor pool make its economy one of the strongest and most promising in the world.

Logging in New Brunswick. Some type of forestry takes place in almost every province. Sawmills and pulp-and-paper plants process the harvest of trees.

Notable Canadians

William Aberhardt, *left* (1878–1943) Founder of the Social Credit party, William Aberhardt began his career as a high school teacher and religious-radio-show host in Calgary, Alberta. During the Great Depression of the 1930s, Aberhardt formed a political party that proposed that the government set fair prices for all goods and that a dividend of $25 be paid by the government to all consumers. Aberhart added his own brand of religious fundamentalism to these radical economic theories, which became popular in Alberta. The Social Credit party controlled the province's legislature until the early 1970s.

Davidialiek Amiituk (born 1910) A carver and printmaker known as Davidialuk, Amiituk grew up in Povungnituk, an Inuit settlement located on the east side of Hudson Bay in Quebec. Amiituk's art is noted for its wild, fantastic mystical imagery. Both his prints and his carvings depict incidents from Inuit mythology.

Denys Arcand (born 1941) A filmmaker from Quebec with strong political interests, Arcand has been writing and directing highly acclaimed documentaries and theatrical films for both television and the cinema since 1962. His work is at once humorous and political in tone, offering distinctive, provocative views of modern Quebec society. *Le Declin de L'Empire Americain* (The Decline of the American Empire) is perhaps his best-known film; it won several prestigious awards in 1986, including the Critic's Prize at the Cannes Film Festival and the New York Film Critics' Best Foreign Film award.

Margaret Atwood

Margaret Atwood (born 1939) Atwood is one of Canada's best-known and most respected contemporary authors. A poet, novelist, and critic, Atwood was first published in 1961. Her poems, stories, and essays examine the difficulties of life in the late 20th century, particularly the plight of the modern woman and her difficult, often ambiguous role in society. Her futuristic novel *The Handmaid's Tale* was published in 1985 and won international critical and popular acclaim. Atwood won the American Humanist of the Year Award in 1987.

Sir Frederick Banting (1891–1941) Born in Newfoundland in 1891, Banting was practicing medicine in London, Ontario, when he began studying the pancreas and its role in human anatomy. He was part of a team that discovered that the pancreas secretes insulin, an essential hormone that helps the body regulate the metabolization of sugar and carbohydrates. Since Banting and his colleagues isolated the hormone, insulin has been used around the world to treat millions of people suffering from diabetes mellitus. For their discovery, Banting and a colleague won the Nobel Prize for physiology. Banting was appointed Canada's first professor of medical research at University of Toronto and was knighted in 1934.

Pierre Berton (born 1920) Born in Whitehorse, Yukon, and educated at the University of British Columbia, Berton worked as a journalist in Vancouver before moving east to Toronto. Since then, Berton has worked as a television journalist and published many highly respected books about Canadian history. His first book, *Klondike*, concerned the Yukon gold rush that made his hometown famous. Another of his books, *Hollywood's Canada*, reveals how Hollywood films have misrepresented or misinterpreted Canadian history. Berton has received 3 Governor-General's Awards and 11 honorary degrees and is a Companion of the Order of Canada.

Baillairgé Family Five generations of this French Canadian family designed and built some of Quebec's most beautiful buildings during the 18th and 19th centuries. Jean, born in 1726, was a master carpenter and architect brought to New France in 1741 by a French bishop. He designed and crafted woodwork for shops, houses, and religious buildings. His son François was born in Quebec in 1759 and is best known for decorating the interior of Notre Dame de la Paix de Quebec and the facade of Notre Dame des Victoires. His nephew Charles helped supervise the construction of Quebec's Parliament Buildings and helped design the terrace and pavilions of the renowned Dufferin Palace. Thomas, born in 1791, helped establish Canada's first set of rules and guidelines for architectural design. His son Charles designed the Université de Laval and the Ottawa Parliament Buildings, among others.

David Blackwood (born 1941) Born in Wesleyville on Bonavista Bay in 1941, Blackwood is one of Newfoundland's best-known visual artists. His prints and paintings focus on the province's unique maritime history, particularly Bonavista Bay's sea captains. Blackwood sees himself as part of the age-old Newfoundland tradition of storytelling; his works are stories told in visual images. Considered one of Canada's most important etchers, Blackwood now lives in Toronto.

J. Armand Bombardier (1907–64) One of Quebec's premier inventors and entrepreneurs, Bombardier is best known for his invention of the snowmobile, an all-terrain vehicle reliable on both soft ground (muskeg) and snow. Naming his invention the Ski-Doo, Bombardier first marketed it in 1959. This motorized vehicle revolutionized life in the Far North by dramatically improving transportation. It also created a new winter sport enjoyed across North America. The Bombardier family still runs Bombardier, Inc., which now makes aerospace components and engines in addition to snowmobiles.

Joseph Brant (1742–1807) Principal chief of the Six Nations Native tribes of New York State during the mid-18th century, Joseph Brant led his people in battle alongside the British against the French during the Seven Years' War and against the Americans during the American Revolution. He was greatly admired as a soldier and was made a captain by the British in 1780. Beginning in 1783, Brant worked to form a united confederation of Iroquois and other western Native Americans to prevent American expansion westward. For their help to the British, Brant and some 1,600 Iroquois were granted land on the Grand River in Ontario.

Étienne Brulé (1592–1633) A dynamic and inspired young lieutenant in the service of explorer Samuel de Champlain, Étienne Brulé was just 17 years old when he was sent to explore the region west of Ontario. He was the first white man to live among the Native people of the region, becoming a skilled interpreter and intermediary between the Europeans and the Huron. Brulé was probably the first European to see lakes Ontario, Huron, and Superior. It is believed that he was eventually killed and eaten by the Huron among whom he lived.

Edith Butler (born 1942) Edith Butler, a singer and composer, grew up the heart of Acadia, the region in eastern Canada that was settled by the French in the 16th and 17th centuries. Through her unique strong voice and distinctive music, this New Brunswick vocal artist has helped to spread Acadian culture throughout the world. She sang at the International Exposition at Osaka, Japan, in 1970 and won the French Académie Charles-Cros Award in 1984. By the late 1980s, Butler had made 11 albums of Acadian songs.

Douglas Joseph Cardinal (born 1934) An architect best known for his masterly design of St. Mary's Church at Red Deer, Alberta, Douglas Cardinal is a Métis (with Native Blackfoot and white ancestry) from Alberta. In designing St. Mary's, Cardinal became the first western Canadian architect to use computers as

Douglas Cardinal

design tools. In addition to his work as a designer, Cardinal has long been involved in Native and Métis political issues. He designed the $93 million Canadian Museum of Civilization in Hull, Quebec, which opened in 1989.

Timothy Eaton (1834–1907) The founder of Canada's largest privately owned department store, Timothy Eaton emigrated from Ireland in 1854. Two years later, he and an older brother opened a small store in Kirkland, Ontario; they later moved the store to Toronto. Eaton revolutionized the way Canadians shopped by introducing mail order. He also vastly improved the working conditions of his employees. At his death in 1907, Eaton's small store had grown into a major conglomerate, employing more than 9,000 people. Today one of Canada's major corporations, the Eaton enterprises remain largely family owned.

Henrietta Louise Edwards (1849–1931) Born to a wealthy Montreal family, Henrietta Edwards became one of Canada's early feminists and political activists. In 1875, she founded the Working Girls' Association to provide vocational training to young women. Later she helped to found two important suffragist organizations, the National Council of Women and the Victorian Order of Nurses. Throughout her life, Edwards worked tirelessly to expand the legal, social, and political rights of women.

Michael J. Fox (born 1961) Born in Edmonton, Alberta, and raised in Burnaby, British Columbia, this television and film actor is best known for his starring role as Alex Keaton in the long-running TV series "Family Ties." Fox's many hit movies include the *Back to the Future* trilogy and the more serious and critically acclaimed *Casualties of War*.

Thomas Forrestall (born 1936) Forrestall is Nova Scotia's best-known artist. His realistic paintings, often done in egg tempera or watercolors, center on the beauty of the Atlantic landscape and its dwellings. He was made an Officer of the Order of Canada in 1986.

Michael J. Fox

Wayne Gretzky

François Xavier Garneau (1809–66) Garneau is widely considered to be both the greatest writer of 19th-century French Canada and its most important historian. He was largely self-educated. His work as a historian began with the three-volume *Histoire du Canada* (History of Canada), which was published in the late 1840s. Garneau presented the history of French Canadians as one of a continual struggle against the British, both on the battlefield and in the political arena. His work is still considered a major source for novelists, poets, and political theorists interested in the history of French Canada.

James Gladstone (1887–1971) Known as Akay-na-muka in his Native Blood language, James Gladstone became Canada's first Native senator when he was appointed to the office in the Northwest Territories in 1958. He spent his life fighting for better treatment of Native Americans, urging improved health care and education and greater respect for treaty rights. He served as president of the Indian Association of Alberta and was frequently a delegate to Ottawa to discuss proposed changes in the Indian Act.

Glenn Gould (1932–82) Before he died suddenly of a stroke at the age of 50, Glenn Gould was known as one of the most brilliant classical pianists of the 20th century. He received his musical education at the Royal Conservatory of Music and was a concert soloist by the time he was 14. His concert and recorded repertoire included all the Bach and Beethoven keyboard works, much Mozart, and works by modern composers such as Hindemith and Schoenberg.

Wayne Gretzky (born 1961) The premier hockey player of the 1980s, Ontario-born Wayne Gretzky became the youngest athlete to play a major-league sport in North America when he signed with the Edmonton Oilers in 1978. In his second National Hockey League season, he scored 164 points, breaking fellow countryman Phil Esposito's single-season record of 152 points; the following year he scored an astounding 212 points. He led the Oilers to win three Stanley Cup titles, in 1983, 1984, and 1987. In this period, the team—and Gretzky himself—shattered practically every NHL point- and goal-scoring record. Gretzky's speed, agility, and accurate shooting have earned him the respect of his colleagues and the admiration of all hockey fans.

Crawford "Buzz" Holling (born 1930) Since becoming a professor of zoology at the University of British Columbia in 1967, this American-born scientist has built an international reputation as an ecologist and forest entomologist. Holling and his colleagues promote strict management of natural resources through workshops and seminars.

Kahn-Tineta Horn (born 1940) A member of the Mohawk Wolf Clan of Caughnawaga, Quebec, Horn—whose name means "she makes the grass wave" in Mohawk—has been a Native rights activist since the 1960s. She was a model and public speaker for many years before taking part in numerous Native rights protests. In 1967, she founded the Indian Legal Defence Committee and served as its director until 1971. Since then, she has held various positions in the federal Department of Indian Affairs.

Gordie Howe (born 1928) Born in Floral, Saskatchewan, Gordie Howe was one of the finest hockey players of all time. Throughout his 32 seasons, most of them with the Detroit Red Wings, he scored more than 1,000 goals, 1,500 assists, and 2,500 points. His career as a professional athlete is one of the longest lasting on record.

René Lévesque (1922–87) Founder of the Parti Québecois, Lévesque was committed to attaining Quebec sovereignty or the creation of a new Canadian constitution recognizing Quebec's special status as a French society. He began his career as a radio and television journalist, then won political office as a member of the Quebec Liberal party in 1960. After serving in a variety of elected and appointed posts, Lévesque left the Liberals to found the Parti Québecois in 1968. In 1976 he became premier when

Kahn-Tineta Horn

the Parti Québecois won a majority of the vote. Lévesque's greatest political defeat came in 1980, when a referendum that would have led Quebec toward independence was soundly defeated. He retired from public service in 1986 and died a year later.

Nellie McClung (1873–1951) Raised on a homestead in Manitoba's Souris Valley, Nellie McClung was a teacher, author, and suffragist during the early and mid-20th century. She first became active in the Women's Christian Temperance Movement in Manitou; later, after moving to Winnipeg, she became a spokeswoman for women's rights, urging woman suffrage. She was a dynamic speaker and gained an international reputation for the speeches she gave in Britain, the United States, and Canada. McClung was also a prolific writer. Her first novel, *Sowing Seeds in Danny*, was published in 1908. A humorous depiction of a quaint Manitoba village, the book became a national best-seller. She wrote more than a dozen volumes of fiction and autobiography.

Marshall McLuhan (1911–80) A professor of English at the University of Toronto, McLuhan studied the effects of mass media—especially television—on thought and behavior. Perhaps his most important contribution to the study of modern communications is his book *The Medium Is the Message*, which describes his theory that the way one receives information—by reading, listening, or watching television—deeply influences one's perception of that information. He published several other books of criticism and theory, including *Through the Vanishing Point* and *Take Today: The Executive as Dropout*. He received numerous North American and European honors.

Mingo Martin (Native name Nakapenkim) (1879–1962) An authority on various aspects of the northwest coast Native cultures, Mingo Martin was a painter, carver, singer, and songwriter. A member of the Kwakiutl people, Martin helped renew pride in his Native culture when he was asked to head a

Canada 8

postes postage
Nellie McClung 1873–1951

A stamp honoring Nellie McClung

project to restore the northwest coast totem poles in 1948. During the 1950s, he helped ethnographers preserve the language and music of the Kwakiutl people by recording some 200 songs at the University of British Columbia. One of Martin's most famous works is the world's tallest totem pole, in Beacon Hill Park, Victoria, completed in 1958.

Joni Mitchell (born 1943) "The Circle Game" and "Both Sides Now" are two of this popular and versatile singer-composer's best-known songs. Mitchell began her career singing folk songs in Calgary and Toronto, eventually moving to Los Angeles, California. Her music has evolved into a unique blend of jazz, folk, and rock rhythms and sounds. *Blue* is generally considered her most influential album. Mitchell has produced some 15 albums since 1968; one of them, *Clouds*, received a Grammy Award in 1969.

Lucy Maud Montgomery (1847–1942) Author of 22 novels and several volumes of short stories, Lucy Maud Montgomery shared the beauty of her native province, Prince Edward Island, with a wide audience. Her most beloved creation was Anne Shirley, heroine of the international best-seller *Anne of Green Gables* and its sequels.

Farley Mowat (born 1921) Considered Canada's most widely read author, Farley Mowat has published nearly 30 books. Since studying biology at the University of Toronto, he has written extensively about man and his relationship to nature. His first book, *People of the Deer* (1952), concerned the problems of the Inuit, which he attributed to the intrusion of white people and their culture into the Arctic. One of his best-known works is *Never Cry Wolf*, which was made into a movie. Mowat's fast-paced yet graceful style continues to attract millions of nature-loving readers around the world.

Joni Mitchell

Lucy Maud Montgomery

Louis Riel

Joseph Smallwood

Peter Pitseolak (1902–73) The intrusion of modern technology into the Arctic north has changed forever the Inuit way of life. This Inuit photographer and artist spent his life trying to preserve and document his people's way of life before it passed into history. He took his first photograph in the 1930s for a white man who was afraid to approach a polar bear and went on to take more than 1,500 photographs of life in the north.

Louis Riel (1844–85) Born near St. Boniface, Manitoba, and educated in Montreal, Riel was a dynamic organizer of the Métis and the founder of the province of Manitoba. In the 1860s he formed an impressive organization of rebellious Métis who fought for land, language, and cultural rights as well as access to political power. In 1869-70, Riel led his men in the Red River Rebellion, which ended when the Manitoba Act created a new Canadian province, called Manitoba, in which the land and cultural rights of Métis were guaranteed. In 1884, at the request of the Métis in Saskatchewan, Riel led a second rebellion against the Canadian government. He was captured and executed. Many Canadians regard Riel as a heroic freedom fighter.

Gabrielle Roy (1909–83) A novelist who depicted working-class life in postwar Canada and the conflict between the values of progress and those of tradition, Roy is considered one of the most important Canadian writers of the late 20th century. Her first novel, *Bonheur d'occasion* (called in English *The Tin Flute*), won the Prix Fémina in Paris and the Literary Guild of America Award in New York. She later published more than a dozen highly acclaimed works of fiction and nonfiction.

Joseph Smallwood (born 1900) Smallwood brought Newfoundland into the Canadian nation. After a career as a journalist, Smallwood turned to politics in 1946 when he was elected to Newfoundland's Confederation Convention. His fierce courage and ruthlessness made him one of Newfoundland's most effective politicians; his support of confederation led the province into the union in 1949. He was then elected as the first provincial premier, a post he held for more than two decades. He commonly described himself as a socialist, and his Liberal party government dramatically expanded Newfoundland's social programs.

Donald Sutherland (born 1935) An internationally acclaimed film actor, Sutherland began his career on the stage, first at the University of Toronto, then in London, England. He has since made dozens of movies in both Canada and the United States, including *M*A*S*H*, *Day of the Locust*, *Ordinary People*, and *Backdraft*.

Pierre Trudeau (born 1919) Canada's 15th prime minister, Pierre Trudeau was born and raised in Montreal. He received his education at the Université de Montreal, Harvard University, the École des Sciences Politiques in Paris, and the London School of Economics. His political career began in 1950, when he helped found *Cité Libre*, a monthly magazine advocating democracy and civil liberties in opposition to the Union National regime of Maurice Duplessis. He entered federal politics as a Liberal in 1965 and was appointed Minister of Justice in 1967. First elected leader of the Liberal party of Canada in 1968, Trudeau served as prime minister for nearly 18 years during some of his nation's most tumultuous times. During his first term, the terrorist organization Front de Libération du Quebec (FLQ), fighting for the rights of French Canadians, kidnapped and murdered Quebec Cabinet minister Pierre Laporte. In response to the growing dissatisfaction of French Canadians, Trudeau's administration oversaw the passage of the Official Languages Act, which ensures the recognition of English and French as Canada's two official languages. In dealing with growing inflation and other economic problems, Trudeau tried to centralize and nationalize decision making—a controversial move that almost cost him his position. In 1980, he worked to defeat the Quebec Referendum, which would have moved Quebec toward independence. Trudeau introduced the Canadian Constitution of 1982. This charismatic leader served longer than any other contemporary leader in the modern Western world.

Pierre Trudeau

Further Reading

Armitage, Peter. *The Innu*. New York: Chelsea House, 1990.

Berton, Pierre. *The Arctic Grail: The Quest for the Northwest Passage and the North Pole*. New York: Viking Penguin, 1988.

———. *Drifting Home*. New York: Knopf, 1974.

———. *Flames Across the Border: 1814*. Toronto: McClelland and Stewart, 1981.

———. *The Impossible Railway: The Building of the Canadian Pacific*. New York: Knopf, 1974.

———. *The Invasion of Canada: 1812–13*. Toronto: McClelland and Stewart, 1980.

Creighton, Donald. *Canada's First Century: 1867–1967*. New York: St. Martin's Press, 1970.

Fingard, Judith. *Jack in Port: Sailortowns of Eastern Canada*. Toronto: University of Toronto Press, 1982.

Francis, R. D., Richard Jones, and D. B. Smith. *Destinies: Canadian History Since Confederation*. Toronto: Holt, Rinehart & Winston, 1988.

———. *Origins: Canadian History to Confederation*. Toronto: Holt, Rinehart & Winston, 1988.

Frideres, James. *Canada's Indians: Contemporary Conflicts*. Englewood Cliffs, NJ: Prentice-Hall, 1974.

Hocking, Anthony. *The Yukon and the Northwest Territories*. New York: McGraw-Hill Ryerson, 1979.

Holbrook, Sabra. *Canada's Kids*. New York: Atheneum, 1983.

Law, Kevin. *Canada*. New York: Chelsea House, 1990.

Lévesque, René. *Memoirs*. Toronto: McClelland and Stewart, 1986.

McNaught, Kenneth. *The Penguin History of Canada*. New York: Penguin Books, 1988.

Malcolm, Andrew. *The Canadians*. New York: Random House, 1985.

Miller, J. R. *Skyscrapers Hide the Heavens: A History of Indian-White Relations in Canada.* Toronto: University of Toronto Press, 1989.

Newman, Peter C. *Caesars of the Wilderness: The Story of the Hudson's Bay Company,* vol II. New York: Penguin Books, 1988.

————. *A Company of Adventurers: The Story of the Hudson's Bay Company,* vol. I. New York: Penguin Books, 1985.

Scott, J. M. *Icebound: Journeys to the Northwest Sea.* London: Gordon and Cremonesi, 1977.

Shephard, Jennifer. *Canada.* Chicago: Childrens Press, 1987.

Smith, P. J., ed. *The Prairie Provinces.* Toronto: University of Toronto Press, 1972.

Statistics Canada. *Canada: A Portrait.* Ottawa: Statistics Canada, 1991.

Taner, Ogden. *The Canadians.* New York: Time-Life Books, 1977.

Wansbrough, M. B. *Great Canadian Lives.* New York: Doubleday, 1986.

Webb, Melody. *The Last Frontier.* Albuquerque: University of New Mexico Press, 1985.

Woodcock, George. *The Canadians.* Cambridge: Harvard University Press, 1979.

————. *The Hudson's Bay Company.* New York: Macmillan, 1970.

————. *A Picture History of British Columbia.* Seattle: University of Washington Press, 1982.

Index

ACKNOWLEDGMENTS

AP/Wide World Photos: pp. 48, 51, 52, 55 (top), 56 (bottom); Map by Diana Blume: pp. 6–7; Courtesy of the Canadian Consulate: pp. 10, 13, 14, 15, 24, 29, 33, 34; Canapress Photo Service: pp. 50, 53, 54, 55 (bottom); Department of Natural Resources and Energy, New Brunswick: p. 45; © 1991 R. Hartmier: pp. 36, 37; © 1991 Wally Hayes: pp. 26, 27; Industry, Science, and Technology Canada: cover, pp. 3, 5, 9, 12, 16, 17, 18, 19, 21, 22, 23, 25, 28, 30, 31, 32, 35, 38, 40, 42, 43; New Brunswick Department of Tourism: p. 20; Notman Photographic Archives, McCord Museum of Canadian History: p. 56 (top); Provincial Archives of Alberta: p. 46; UPI/ Bettmann Archive: pp. 39, 57

Suzanne LeVert has contributed several volumes to Chelsea House's LET'S DISCOVER CANADA series. She is the author of four previous books for young readers. One of these, *The Sakharov File*, a biography of noted Russian physicist Andrei Sakharov, was selected as a Notable Book by the National Council for the Social Studies. Her other books include *AIDS: In Search of a Killer*, *The Doubleday Book of Famous Americans*, and *New York*. Ms. LeVert also has extensive experience as an editor, first in children's books at Simon & Schuster, then as associate editor at *Trialogue*, the magazine of the Trilateral Commission, and as senior editor at Save the Children, the international relief and development organization. She lives in Cambridge, Massachusetts.

George Sheppard, General Editor, is a lecturer on Canadian and American history at McMaster University in Hamilton, Ontario. Dr. Sheppard holds an honors B.A. and an M.A. in history from Laurentian University and earned his Ph.D. in Canadian history at McMaster. He has taught Canadian history at Nipissing University in North Bay. His research specialty is the War of 1812, and he has published articles in *Histoire sociale/Social History*, *Papers of the Bibliographical Society of Canada*, and *Ontario History*. Dr. Sheppard is a native of Timmins, Ontario.

Pierre Berton, Senior Consulting Editor, is the author of 34 books, including *The Mysterious North*, *Klondike*, *Great Canadians*, *The Last Spike*, *The Great Railway Illustrated*, *Hollywood's Canada*, *My Country: The Remarkable Past*, *The Wild Frontier*, *The Invasion of Canada*, *Why We Act Like Canadians*, *The Klondike Quest*, and *The Arctic Grail*. He has won three Governor General's Awards for creative nonfiction, two National Newspaper Awards, and two ACTRA "Nellies" for broadcasting. He is a Companion of the Order of Canada, a member of the Canadian News Hall of Fame, and holds 12 honorary degrees. Raised in the Yukon, Mr. Berton began his newspaper career in Vancouver. He then became managing editor of *McLean's*, Canada's largest magazine, and subsequently worked for the Canadian Broadcasting Network and the *Toronto Star*. He lives in Kleinburg, Ontario.